BOY SCOUTS OF AMERICA
MERIT BADGE SERIES

CRIME PREVENTION

BOY SCOUTS OF AMERICA®

Requirements

1. Discuss the role and value of laws in society with regard to crime and crime prevention. Include in your discussion the definitions of "crime" and "crime prevention."

2. Prepare a notebook of newspaper and other clippings that address crime and crime prevention efforts in your community.

3. Discuss the following with your counselor:

   a. The role of citizens, including youth, in crime prevention.

   b. Gangs and their impact on the community.

   c. When and how to report a crime.

4. After doing EACH of the following, discuss with your counselor what you have learned.

   a. Inspect your neighborhood for opportunities that may lead to crime. Learn how to do a crime prevention survey.

   b. Using the checklist in this pamphlet, conduct a security survey of your home and discuss the results with your family.

5. Teach your family or patrol members how to protect themselves from crime at home, at school, in your community, and while traveling.

35880
ISBN 978-0-8395-3400-6
©2005 Boy Scouts of America
2008 Printing

6. Help raise awareness about one school safety issue facing students by doing ONE of the following:

   a. Create a poster for display on a school bulletin board.

   b. With permission from school officials, create a pagelong public service announcement that could be read over the public address system at school or posted on the school's Web site.

   c. Make a presentation to a group such as a Cub Scout den that addresses the issue.

7. Do ONE of the following:

   a. Assist in the planning and organization of a crime prevention program in your community such as Neighborhood Watch, Community Watch, or Crime Stoppers. Explain how this program can benefit your neighborhood.

   b. With your parent's and counselor's approval, visit a jail or detention facility or a criminal court hearing. Discuss your experience with your counselor.

8. Discuss the following with your counselor:

   a. How drug abuse awareness programs such as "Drugs: A Deadly Game" help prevent crime.

   b. Why alcohol, tobacco, and marijuana are sometimes called "gateway drugs" and how gateway drugs can lead to the use of other drugs.

   c. Three resources in your city where a person with a drug problem or drug-related problem can go for help.

   d. How the illegal sale and use of drugs lead to other crimes.

   e. How to recognize child abuse.

   f. The three R's of Youth Protection.

9. Discuss the following with your counselor:

   a. The role of a sheriff's or police department in crime prevention.

   b. The purpose and operation of agencies in your community that help law enforcement personnel prevent crime, and how those agencies function during emergency situations.

   c. Explain the role private security plays in crime prevention.

   d. Choose a career in the crime prevention or security industry that interests you. Describe the level of education required and responsibilities of a person in that position. Tell why this position interests you.

Contents

Police
and
Neighborhood:
A Partnership!

Come to BSA Troop 468
neighborhood watch meeting
this Monday night at Troop
468 scout hut 7pm

Find out how we can help our
neighborhood and find out
about crime prevention

Introduction

Every citizen is affected by crime. Millions of crimes are reported to law enforcement agencies every year and these acts affect you and your family either directly or indirectly.

Crime is the violation of a law, a duty, or a moral principle. Those arrested by law enforcement officers for committing crimes face prosecution and punishment. In this pamphlet, you will learn about the different types of crimes and steps that you, and your family and neighbors, can take to help prevent crime.

In addition to being possible victims of crime, your family and other citizens carry the financial burden of criminal acts. Citizens must pay, usually through higher taxes, for additional law enforcement officers, increased court costs, and more prisons and jails. Because retail stores must recoup their losses from theft and robbery, consumers also pay more for goods when owners raise prices to cover their losses.

Citizens also pay a price when companies and governments are victimized by less obvious criminal acts, such as theft by employees. Some of these illegal activities involving national or worldwide companies can be far-reaching and create huge financial losses for consumers.

Identity theft is a growing problem, too. This is when criminals gain access to someone's credit card number or some other kind of personal identification. Criminals then use this information for illegal financial gains.

Internet Safety

These tips will help you stay safe and protect your identity when surfing the Internet. Before you log on to the Internet, make sure you have a parent's permission. Your parents, counselor, or librarian might discuss other precautions with you.

1. Follow your family's rules for using the Internet. Respect the limits they set for how long and how often you are allowed to be online and what sites you can visit. Your family also can consider installing a software program that helps weed out undesirable sites.

2. Protect your privacy. Never exchange electronic pictures of yourself with strangers, and never give out personal information or any other identification, such as your phone number, address, last name, where you go to school, or where your parents work, without first asking your parent's permission.

3. Do not open e-mail or files you receive from people or businesses you do not know or trust. If you get something suspicious, put it in the trash just as you would any other electronic junk mail, which is known as spam. Many computer viruses are sent via e-mail attachments. You should have updated virus protection software and, especially with cable or DSL connections, a firewall. A firewall will help prevent a hacker from obtaining information from your computer or placing information and viruses on it.

4. If you receive or discover any information that makes you uncomfortable, tell your parents and let them look at it. Do not respond to any message that is disturbing or hurtful.

5. Never agree to get together with someone you meet online, unless your parents approve of the meeting and go with you.

6. Never share your Internet password with anyone other than your parents or other responsible adults in your family. Sometimes a fraudulent e-mail will appear official and request personal information.

7. Never shop online or offer a credit card number unless you have your parent's permission.

8. Besides having an abundance of useful and accurate information, the Internet also has its dark side, including misinformation. Talk with your counselor or other experienced Internet users about ways to tell the difference.

9. Be a good online citizen. Do not do anything that harms others or is against the law. Be aware that information you provide such as notes and personal remarks may be shared with others. A good rule of thumb is to not post information you don't want others, including strangers, to see.

Crime prevention is defined by law enforcement agencies as "the anticipation, recognition, and appraisal of a crime risk and the initiation of some action to remove or reduce the risk."

City, state, and federal governments work to apprehend and bring legal action against those who break the law. Because of the amount of work, equipment, and personnel involved, these agencies spend millions of dollars. Preventing crime is less costly to citizens and society and helps save people from the anguish of being victims.

If someone wants to commit a crime, there must be an opportunity to do so. Therefore, many crimes can be prevented by reducing or eliminating opportunities.

Citizens need to work with law enforcement agents to avoid becoming victims and to help prevent crime. Crime prevention by citizens is not vigilantism. Vigilantes are those who take the law into their own hands, which is wrong.

Preparing a Crime Prevention Notebook

A good way to become informed about crime in your neighborhood is to start a notebook. Clip and save articles from newspapers and other sources relating to crime and crime prevention in your area. Talk to neighbors and watch or listen to the news about crimes and crime prevention. Write down useful information to add to your notebook.

One of the first steps in crime prevention is being aware of the types of crimes being committed in your community. Your notebook probably will have articles that mention many of these crimes.

Burglary. Breaking into and entering a building with the intent of committing a crime, often by stealing something.

Robbery. Taking someone else's property unlawfully, by force or fear.

Larceny. Unlawfully removing the personal goods of another person with the intent to cheat the owner. Also known as theft.

Crimes against people. These crimes include murder, robbery, assault, and rape.

Crimes against property. These crimes include burglary, larceny, motor-vehicle theft, arson, and vandalism.

White-collar crime. This term, coined more than 60 years ago, now includes a variety of nonviolent crimes committed for the financial benefit of one or more persons. This could include embezzlement as well as fraud, computer hacking, and theft of office supplies and equipment.

Embezzlement is the act of stealing money or property that has been entrusted to one's care. Fraud includes tricking or cheating someone for profit or to gain an unfair advantage. Computer hacking includes using a personal computer to gain unauthorized access to valuable private information.

White-collar crime made the headlines at the turn of the 21st century when executives at several large companies were accused of insider stock trading, falsifying company earnings reports, and using company money in inappropriate ways.

Insider trading means that an officer or some employee at a publicly owned company either sells or buys the company's stock based on knowledge that other stockholders do not have. This information also may be passed along to friends or business associates so they can either buy or sell the stock before the general public and other stockholders become aware of the development.

When these schemes are discovered, the stocks of these companies usually plummet and often cause shareholders and company employees to lose thousands of dollars. Many lose their entire investments.

Littering. Many people litter without thinking. How many times have you seen people throw out cups, paper, cans, and cigarette butts from their car windows? They are showing disrespect for neighborhoods and other people. Litter can be harmful to plants and animals, depending on how the trash decomposes. Also, fragments from plastic and glass can harm animals and people if they step on them.

Your troop can organize and take part in community cleanups. Encourage store owners to put trash cans near entrances and exits. Conveniently located waste receptacles are especially important for stores selling products that are packaged in wrappers or containers. The trash cans should be emptied regularly.

Cigarettes are the most littered item in the world. The filters, made of cellulose acetate, take decades to degrade. Cigarettes also can ignite a fire, especially during dry months. These fires can be devastating and deadly.

Graffiti needs to be cleaned up as soon as possible.

Graffiti. Many of us associate graffiti-covered buildings and bridges with high-crime neighborhoods and uncaring residents. We may not consider it important in our own community. But in addition to possibly igniting gang violence, graffiti makes neighborhood property less valuable and makes people feel unsafe. It also can make a negative impression on visitors.

Report any graffiti to your local law enforcement agency.

In some neighborhoods, especially in big cities, graffiti is the work of gang members, who use it to mark their territories.

Shoplifting. This crime deprives the store owner of both the merchandise and the profit from selling it. Thus, many store owners might have to raise the prices on other goods to offset the stolen merchandise.

It is almost impossible to spot a shoplifter in a crowd because there is not just one kind of person who commits this crime. Many shoplifters are well-dressed and have enough money to pay for the items they steal.

There are three basic types of shoplifters: the average citizen, the full-time amateur, and the professional. The average-citizen shoplifter accounts for about 75 percent of shoplifting. About 20 percent of shoplifters are full-time amateurs. Professional shoplifters make up only 5 percent of shoplifters, but they steal a much higher quality and quantity of goods. Many of these people steal to pay for drug habits. After they steal the merchandise, they sell it cheaply. Professionals usually work in pairs and travel widely.

Something for Nothing

Shoplifters might start out wanting to get something for nothing, but once caught, they find themselves getting something they might not have expected. About 25 percent of apprehended shoplifters are juveniles ages 13 to 17, and *nearly all juvenile shoplifters are caught.* Retailers are more likely than ever to prosecute all thieves—no matter how small the "take" or whether it is a first-time offense—and hold them accountable for their behavior. To the juvenile petty thief, this may mean the police will go to the offender's school, question friends, and talk with parents and neighbors. Some first-time offenders are lucky. Their community might have a program to help them make better choices in the future.

Many stores have low profit margins, and they suffer when someone shoplifts as little as $2. For example, if a store has a profit margin of 10 percent and someone steals an item that costs $2, then the store owner must sell $20 worth of merchandise to offset the loss.

Police and Citizens: Working Together

Citizens, including you and other young people, are responsible for the quality of life in their communities. Law enforcement officers help keep the community safe, and they often rely on cooperation from citizens in their crime prevention efforts. Police are trained to enforce the law and to give citizens information to help prevent crime.

It is up to citizens to protect their personal property, help neighbors guard their property, and report to the police any crime or suspicious activities. Citizens also can establish programs within the community, such as Neighborhood Watch, to help deter criminals.

Citizens can help prevent crime by cooperating not only with law enforcement officers, but also with prosecutors and courts in the criminal justice process. For those people who do not obey laws and who might harm others through their actions, it is up to law-abiding citizens to help thwart their actions. Citizens have a duty to work with the justice system to help identify, capture, and prosecute (bring legal action against) lawbreakers.

It is sometimes easy to ignore acts of crime when they do not directly affect you or your family. However, when someone you know becomes a victim of a crime, you begin to realize the serious effects of crime and the importance of prevention. Remember, no one is immune from crime.

A Scout obeys the laws of his community and country. Because laws are designed to protect you and all citizens, it is important for you to learn about laws, to obey them, and to recognize the need to work for their improvement when they need improvement. By knowing, respecting, and obeying laws, you can help make your neighborhood, city, state, and nation better and safer places to live.

Gangs and Crime

Among the growing crime concerns in many neighborhoods are gangs, gang violence, and the use and trafficking of drugs. Gangs frequently include teenagers. To support their interests, gangs often commit violent offenses, cause serious injuries, and use lethal weapons.

Gangs can make neighborhoods unsafe and increase security costs for businesses in those areas. Other costs to citizens could be the devaluation of their property because of living in an undesirable neighborhood.

The National Youth Gang Center estimates that there are more than 650,000 members in more than 25,000 gangs in the United States. However, it is difficult to get an accurate count because law enforcement agencies have many different methods of reporting gangs, and because many rural communities are not included in these tallies. Nevertheless, gangs pose a serious threat and are responsible for much of the nation's crime.

Characteristics of a gang may include:

- Links to a neighborhood or territory or ethnicity
- Identifiable leadership
- Members who regularly interact with one another
- Formal organization
- Harmful or violent behavior

> **Young people join gangs for many reasons, including academic failure and family or peer-group pressure.**

Teenagers who join gangs and then decide it was not such a good idea often have a rude awakening when they try to quit. Not only do fellow gang members make quitting tough for them—sometimes even dangerous—but by then these youths have established a reputation for being a member of a gang. Such a stigma can be difficult (but not impossible) to shake.

Gang violence is not limited to gang members. Innocent bystanders often are victims of gang violence. Here are some suggestions for how you can protect yourself from violent crime:

- Do not use alcohol or other drugs. Stick with friends who are not violent and who do not use alcohol or drugs. Avoid known trouble spots and difficult situations.

- Settle arguments with words, not fists or weapons. Do not stand and watch while others are arguing because violence often spreads to bystanders.

- Learn safe routes and good places to find help in your neighborhood. If you sense danger, get away fast. Report any crimes, suspicious actions, or suspicious people to law enforcement officers, school authorities, or your parents.

- Whenever you leave home, tell your parents, relatives, or other responsible adults where you are going, with whom, and when you expect to be home.

- Help teach younger children how to avoid being victims of crime. Set a good example.

- Follow the Scout Oath and Law in your daily life.

Since 1994, the rate of juvenile crime has decreased. Government officials attribute the decline to a reduction in the use of crack cocaine and the number of violent gangs that peddle it. Police crackdowns on illegal guns and expanded after-school crime prevention programs also have helped curb juvenile crime.

The BSA's Venturing program is a great way for youth to be involved in worthwhile activities with good friends.

One of the best solutions to the gang problem is for youngsters to become members in worthwhile youth groups, such as the Boy Scouts of America, that provide opportunity, fun, and peer approval. Other programs that involve youths include the Boys and Girls Clubs of America, PAL (Police Activities League), YMCA, and the Juvenile Mentoring Program.

Reporting Crimes

Besides recognizing the types of crime in your neighborhood, it is important to know how to report a crime should you witness or know about one.

It is essential to law enforcement and to your community that all crimes be reported accurately and promptly. Prompt reports are vital in solving crimes. If a crime is committed against you or any member of your family, or if you see a crime, be sure to report it immediately. The information you have might give law enforcement officers the last piece in the puzzle of catching a criminal, establishing a pattern or method, or preventing future crimes.

You might feel it is embarrassing to admit that you have been a victim. Your family might be tempted to avoid publicity and simply file an insurance claim for any losses in an effort to be rid of the problem. However, your silence might allow a criminal to go on committing crimes. This approach could worsen the problem because that same criminal could be injuring others or damaging the overall quality of life in your community.

A better choice is to report any crime or suspected crime to your local law enforcement officers. It is their responsibility to assist you, investigate, and, if probable cause exists, to file charges and follow the case through the courts. When citizens use this process, criminals have less of an opportunity to commit the same crime in the future because you have set a good example and helped to bring criminals to justice.

You should have emergency and other helpful numbers posted in a convenient place or near every phone in your house for easy access. Look in the blue pages or "helpful numbers" section of your local phone book to find listings for organizations that are involved in preventing, reporting, or responding to crime.

Probable cause means that there's a good reason to believe a crime has occurred.

Emergency Telephone Numbers

EMERGENCY
Police, Fire, or Ambulance
911

Poison Control 1-800-222-1212	Pharmacy 214-555-1098
Nonemergency Police 214-555-0082	Grandma 214-555-7105
Family Doctor: Dr. Bradford 214-555-8632	Mr. Johnson (our neighbor) 214-555-8903
Dentist: Dr. Chang 214-555-7654	Yale Elementary School 214-555-4069

If you call the police department to report a crime, you will talk to a dispatcher. Explain to the dispatcher why you are calling. If it's decided that an officer should be sent to your location, try to remain calm as you wait. Do not hang up the phone until police have arrived or you have been instructed to do so by the dispatcher. Wait for the police. For crimes in progress or if your life is in danger, immediately call 9-1-1 rather than the police number.

Inspecting Your Neighborhood

Studies have shown that crime can decrease by as much as 20 percent in well-lit neighborhoods.

Opportunities for crime can and must be eliminated or reduced. Look around your neighborhood to see what can be done to help prevent crime. Take a notebook and conduct a crime survey of your neighborhood by creating a checklist of possible problems. Go with a parent or counselor when conducting the survey.

Among things to look for are abandoned buildings with broken windows, burned-out or broken street lights, overgrown bushes, and unusual activities at certain residences or abandoned buildings. These residences or buildings could be used by criminals to hide or sell drugs or stolen goods. Unusual activities could be different cars or people visiting a house or building at odd hours and for brief periods of time. This could indicate that drugs or stolen merchandise are being sold.

Eliminating or trimming bushes effectively reduces hiding places for criminals.

Operation Identification is a program that involves marking personal property with unique numbers to make identification possible if the items are lost or stolen. This program aids police in identifying your valuables. People who mark their properties have a better chance of getting them back if they are stolen. Operation I.D. also deters burglars by making it more difficult to sell stolen goods and by increasing the burglar's chances of being arrested.

Numbers can be engraved onto metal objects or marked with indelible markers on other materials. Some police departments recommend using a driver's license number. Contact your local police department to find out more about this program. Many police and sheriff's offices have engraving pens available for you to borrow. Engraving pens also can be purchased in hardware stores. Make a list of all your valuable items, including a description and any serial numbers. It is also recommended that you take a photograph or video of the items. Operation I.D. would be a good community service project for your Scout troop.

Home Security Awareness

Government statistics show that burglaries have declined over the past several years. However, it is estimated that one in six homes is burglarized every year.

Most burglaries are committed by beginners, and the typical burglar is a male teenager who lives either in or near the neighborhood. Burglaries most often occur between 10 A.M. and 3 P.M. because those are the hours when families usually are away from home.

Check your house to see how easy or difficult it would be to break in. Especially check the windows, garage doors, and front and back doors. Burglars usually enter a home through windows and doors. A burglar wants to break in quickly to avoid being seen. The more difficult it is to pry open a door or window, the better chance the burglar will leave and seek an easier target.

Avoid keeping all the family's valuables in the master bedroom because that usually is the first place a burglar will search. Check to see if there are places outside the home where burglars could hide when trying to break into your home. Bushes, trees or anything else that could provide a shield for a burglar should be removed or trimmed.

Home Security Checklist

Survey your home, using the following checklist. Every "no" answer shows a weak point that might help a burglar. As you and your family eliminate the "no" answers, you improve your home and personal security.

  Yes ☑ No

1. Do you keep a list of all valuable property?

   Make the list in duplicate, with at least one copy kept in a place outside your home, such as a safe-deposit box. In case of fire, the extra list that you keep will provide information necessary for insurance claims.

 ☐ Yes ☑ No

2. Do you have a list of the serial numbers of your valuable property, such as TVs, computers, DVDs, audio and video components, cameras, watches, etc.?

 ☑ Yes ☐ No

3. Do you keep excess cash and other valuables in a bank?

   Renting a safe-deposit box is a small investment compared with the potential loss from theft or fire. The box should be large enough to hold important papers and valuables that are seldom used. Copies of valuable papers also could be kept with another family member or relative.

4. Do you leave the spare house key with a close friend or reliable neighbor when you go out of town?　☐ Yes　☐ No

Sometimes

This practice is much safer than leaving a spare under the doormat, where a nosy burglar is certain to look.

5. Do your family members know what to do if they discover a burglar breaking into or already in your home?　☐ Yes　☐ No

If you find signs that your home has been entered, stay out-side. Use your mobile phone, or use a neighbor's phone to call the police or sheriff. If you enter your home and find a burglar inside, expect the burglar to be frightened and dangerous. A scream might cause a burglar to flee, but it might also provoke an attack. Never struggle with a burglar unless you are forced to defend yourself. In that case, scream, kick, gouge—use your hands, feet, and teeth to fend off your attacker.

6. Do family members know to leave everything undisturbed and call the sheriff or police if they discover that a burglary has been committed?　☐ Yes　☐ No

You should not move things or otherwise disturb the inside of your home or the grounds around your home until police have checked it. Otherwise, valuable evidence might be lost.

7. Are trees and shrubs trimmed to eliminate hiding places?　☐ Yes　☐ No

Keep doorways, windows, and porches clear when plant-ing bushes and tall flowers. Remember that the bushes that give you privacy also give a burglar places to hide.

8. Do you have a security closet with a solid-core door, nonremovable hinges, and a deadbolt lock?　☐ Yes　☐ No

A security closet can be a place to keep things of value. Noises caused by someone breaking into a security closet might betray a burglar.

9. Do you have emergency telephone numbers listed on your phone or in an easily accessible place?　☐ Yes　☐ No

In most areas of the country, the 9-1-1 telephone number will connect you with emergency services. With the 9-1-1 system, a computer immediately displays your address to the person who answers your emergency call.

☐ Yes ☐ No   10. Is the outside of your home well-lit?

☐ Yes ☐ No   11. Does your porch light have at least a 60-watt bulb?

Outside lighting is important in home security. Light yards, windows, and doorways to prevent burglars from hiding there. Porch lamps and yard post lamps can be used to eliminate dark spots. Burn porch lights from dusk until dawn, and encourage neighbors to do the same. This denies burglars the cover of darkness, at a cost of about 5 cents per night, using a 60-watt bulb. In rural areas where no streetlights exist, electric companies often will give group discounts to customers who wish to install security lighting. Contact your power company or rural electric cooperative for further information.

☐ Yes ☐ No   12. Is your house number (address) easily visible from the street at any hour?

If it is not possible to read your house number from the street at night without using a flashlight, consider lighting the number or having a visible curb number painted in front of your house.

Nothing is more frustrating to police officers responding to a call for help than to have trouble finding the right house because the house number is not visible. Every house on a street should have a number that is uniform in size and location and visible at night.

A good troop project would be a house-numbering service to ensure that all house numbers in your neighborhood are uniform and easily seen.

13. Have you made it more difficult for burglars by locking up ladders and eliminating trellises and drainpipes that can be climbed to reach an upper floor of your home, if you have one?   ☐ Yes   ☐ No

14. Are your doors of solid-core construction?   ☐ Yes   ☐ No

    A hollow-core door is fragile. It takes a burglar only a few blows with a hammer to break through to reach the lock. If you have hollow-core doors, consider replacing them with solid doors.

15. Do your entry doors have wide-angle viewers or peepholes?   ☐ Yes   ☐ No

    A wide-angle viewer or peephole lets you see who the visitor is before you open the door.

16. Are the locks on your doors secure from being opened if a burglar breaks out a pane of glass or a panel of light-weight wood?   ☐ Yes   ☐ No

    This calls for a lock that can be opened only from inside with a key. Some communities do not permit this type of lock because it can prevent escape from a fire if the key is not in place. If you use this type of lock, be sure to leave the key in the lock when anyone is at home; remove the key only when the home is empty. Check with your local law enforcement agency or building department to find out if this type of lock is permitted.

17. Do exterior doors have cylinder-type deadbolt locks with at least a 1-inch throw and a beveled cylinder guard?   ☐ Yes   ☐ No

18. Do doors without cylinder locks have a heavy deadbolt or some similar security device that can be operated only from the inside?   ☐ Yes   ☐ No

19. Can all of your doors (basement, porch, sliding, French, balcony) be securely locked?   ☐ Yes   ☐ No

20. If you have a basement, do the doors have locks that allow you to isolate that part of your home?   ☐ Yes   ☐ No

    Basement windows are among the easiest for a burglar to enter undetected. If your basement is securely locked from the rest of your home, the burglar's activity is limited to that area.

☐ Yes ☐ No   21. Are all of your locks in good repair?

☐ Yes ☐ No   22. Are the door strike plates installed with 3-inch screws?

                 This size screw will reach the stud inside the wall.

Installing Security Devices

Using the contributed services of repair people or maintenance workers in your neighborhood is a great way to help your neighbors install locks, window pins and bars, peepholes, and other security devices. Donated help saves the cost of installation and encourages more citizens to take important security measures.

     Neighborhood groups might arrange to purchase locks and other security devices in quantity at a discount. Local authorities might install security devices at little cost to residents. Some residents, including senior citizens, persons with disabilities, and burglary victims, might receive services for free.

☐ Yes ☐ No   23. Do you know everyone who has a key to your home?

             Do not carry house keys on the same ring as car keys. It is very easy to leave the keys together when the car is in a garage for repairs or left in a commercial parking lot where an attendant parks cars. Anyone who handles your house keys can easily have duplicates made.

☐ Yes ☐ No   24. Do all out-swinging doors in your home have hinges with nonremovable pins? These hinges have set screws to prevent pin removal from the outside.

☐ Yes ☐ No   25. Do sliding doors have a lock that locks both the door panels together or locks the active side to the frame?

             You can place a wooden dowel in the floor track to prevent a sliding door from opening.

26. Is the garage door secured with a padlock, hasp, or other good lock? ☐ Yes ☐ No

Even garage doors with electric openers need separate locks. In a double-car garage with a single long door, it's important to place a lock on each side of the door to keep a burglar from pulling out one side and crawling through.

27. Do you lock your garage door at night? ☐ Yes ☐ No

28. Do you make sure your garage door is locked when you are away from home? ☐ Yes ☐ No

29. Do you lock your car and take out the keys even when it is parked in your garage? ☐ Yes ☐ No

30. Are all windows in your home equipped with key locks or pinned? ☐ Yes ☐ No

You can secure a sliding window with a rod the same way as you would secure a sliding glass door.

31. Are your window locks properly and securely mounted? ☐ Yes ☐ No

32. Do you keep your windows locked when they are shut? ☐ Yes ☐ No

33. Do you use locks that let you lock a window that is partly open? ☐ Yes ☐ No

34. Have you replaced or secured louvered windows? ☐ Yes ☐ No

35. If you live in a high-burglary area, do you use window bars or ornamental grilles? ☐ Yes ☐ No

Take care that bars or grilles do not create an escape hazard in the event of a fire. They must have an inside mechanism that allows them to swing out in an emergency.

36. Do you have secure locks on garage windows? ☐ Yes ☐ No

37. Do you cover garage windows with curtains or shades? ☐ Yes ☐ No

38. Are you as careful to secure basement and second-story windows as you are to secure windows on the first floor? ☐ Yes ☐ No

39. Do you use good telephone security procedures? ☐ Yes ☐ No

Telephone Security

- Never give personal information (name, age, address, etc.) to a stranger on the telephone.

- Never let a stranger know that you are home alone.

- Never let strangers on the telephone know when you will or will not be home.

- Instruct babysitters never to tell anyone who calls that they are home alone with children.

- Teach children who are old enough to answer the phone never to tell a stranger on the phone that parents are gone. Teach them to say, "My mom (or dad) is busy. May I take a message?"

☐ Yes   ☐ No   40. When planning a trip, do you secure your telephone?

Use an answering machine or voice mail service from the telephone company to record a message indicating all calls will be returned at your earliest convenience. You can then call home and retrieve your messages without anyone knowing you are away. Never say that you are out of town.

☐ Yes   ☐ No   41. When you go on a trip, do you arrange for someone to collect newspapers, mail, packages, and other deliveries?

You also can request the post office and newspaper to stop delivery until you return.

☐ Yes   ☐ No   42. Do you arrange to make your home look lived-in while you are away?

Leave some window shades up or curtains open so that your home does not look deserted. Have a trusted neighbor or relative periodically open and close drapes and turn different lights on and off (or use timers) so that the house appears occupied. You can also use a timer to turn a radio and/or light on and off. Consider asking friends or relatives to live in your home while you are away. Leave a car in the driveway or ask neighbors to park in your driveway. Ask a neighbor to put some trash in your trash cans, place them out for pick up on trash days, and pick them up after they have been emptied.

43. Do you notify a trusted neighbor that you will be gone? ☐ Yes ☐ No

44. Do you notify your police or sheriff's department that you will be gone? ☐ Yes ☐ No

45. Do you store all your valuables in a secure place while you are gone, such as a safe-deposit box in a bank? ☐ Yes ☐ No

Apartment Precautions

There are special precautions to take if your family lives in an apartment.

- Always tell trusted neighbors and the apartment manager when you will be away for an extended period.

- Does your apartment management monitor who enters and leaves the building? If not, consider starting an apartment watch group that helps monitor people entering and leaving. An apartment watch group could start a tenant patrol.

- Walkways, parking areas, hallways, laundry rooms, and storage areas should be among the places that are well-lit at all times.

- Mailboxes should be in a well-lit area and have good locks.

- Get to know your neighbors.

- Work with the manager to make safety changes around the apartments (trim bushes, for example) and to assure safety at playgrounds and other areas.

Safety When You Travel

Remind your parents that before going on a trip or even when driving around town, they need to keep the car in good repair. That means they should keep the gas tank full, have properly inflated tires, and keep the car in good running order. Before trips, the car should be checked by a mechanic for possible problems, such as worn fan belts. You and your family do not want the family vehicle to break down, especially in unfamiliar, undesirable, or desolate places.

When driving, stay on well-lit, well-traveled roads. Select your route ahead of time and become familiar with it to lessen the chances of getting lost. Avoid high-crime areas, even if it means going out of your way. If your family is a member of an auto service club, you can obtain a map that usually shows the best route to take. You also can obtain maps and directions on the Internet. Study the routes and make sure you avoid going through undesirable places.

Here are some other tips to remain safe while traveling:

- Always check inside and underneath your car before getting in to make sure no one is hiding there.

- If you keep your car in a garage, make sure to lock the door as you leave.

- Always keep the garage door closed, whether you are away or at home.

- When the vehicle is on the road or parked, keep all the doors and windows locked.

- Park in attended lots when possible, especially in a strange area.

- If it is necessary to leave a key with an attendant, leave only the valet key.

- Keep all packages or personal items out of view in the car—preferably in the trunk, and try to place them there when no one is looking.

- At night, park only in lighted areas and take note of your surroundings so you will notice any changes when you return.

- If it appears that you are in a dangerous situation and could be harmed or robbed while in your car, lock your doors and sound the horn until help arrives. After sounding the horn, use your cell phone, if you have one, to call an emergency number.

- Never pick up a hitchhiker or a motorist next to a stalled car, no matter how friendly or harmless the person appears. You can call police to help the motorist.

- If you have a flat tire in an unsafe area, try to keep driving until reaching a safe location. Ruining a tire and/or wheel might be cheap compared with what could happen.

- If you believe a car is following you, drive to a police or fire station. If there is not a station nearby, go to an open service/gas station or business and signal for help. Do not go to your home or, if you are out of town, your hotel or motel. You also could sound your horn until the car leaves or someone comes to your assistance.

- If a car intentionally blocks your path, lock your doors, sound the horn repeatedly, and do not leave your vehicle. Park as close as possible to your destination.

- Pay attention when you return to your vehicle. If you see someone waiting near it, walk past and find help.

- If your car breaks down, signal and pull onto the shoulder of the road. Turn on the emergency flashers and tie a cloth to the driver's door handle or to the antenna. If you have reflective material, wave it or use some other signaling device. Call for assistance if you have a cell phone. If some-one other than a uniformed law enforcement officer stops, roll down the window only enough to ask the person to call the police, auto club, or service station.

School Safety

Schools are not immune from crime. To see if and how crime might be affecting your school, visit your principal, teachers, and school security officer. Ask what measures they have taken to reduce crime. For example, has your school started any after-school programs? Research and crime-fighting experience by law enforcement agencies have shown that good after-school programs can be a key element in fighting juvenile crime. Reports by these agencies have shown that when youngsters are without constructive after-school activities or adult supervision, the rate of violent juvenile crime increases.

Crime Awareness at School

Help your classmates become more aware of crime at school by creating a poster that reflects some of the safety issues students face during a typical school day. Among subjects you might consider would be gang violence and drug issues. The poster could include clippings from newspapers and magazines. You could exhibit this poster at your school, with your principal's or teacher's permission.

As an alternative, consider creating a pagelong public service announcement that could be read over your school's public address system or posted on the school's Web site. You will need permission from your principal or other school official.

Consider sharing your poster or presentation with your troop or a Cub Scout pack.

Neighborhood Watch

Neighborhood Watch, Block Watch, and Town Watch are programs designed to prevent crime. They help neighborhoods enhance home and personal security and reduce fear and isolation. Civic involvement has helped cities and neighborhoods to significantly reduce crime.

In early 1972, the National Sheriffs' Association created a model program for today's Neighborhood Watch. The program, among other things, forges strong bonds among residents.

To start a Neighborhood Watch program in your area, you first will need to help your parents conduct a survey of residents and business owners. Ask them about their concerns, such as worries about burglaries or other crimes, and their willingness to work for their neighborhood. Have they done anything to protect their homes or businesses? Would they be willing to attend a meeting to organize a Neighborhood Watch group? Create a list of the people you survey and those who are interested in joining a neighborhood or block watch. Include their addresses and telephone numbers. Establish a planning committee of people who are interested.

Next, contact your local law enforcement agency. Request that a crime prevention officer attend a meeting of neighbors to discuss community needs, the level of interest, and local crime problems. Schedule a date, time, and place for a Neighborhood Watch kickoff meeting.

> Residents should be aware of possible terrorist activities. The Neighborhood Watch program has been expanded to include USAonwatch and the Citizen Corps, terrorism prevention and response programs.

Planning a Successful First Meeting

To ensure a successful first meeting, get help from existing communities that have a Neighborhood Watch or Block Watch program. Their bylaws and mission statements might make good models for your group. Have your planning committee schedule the first meeting in a convenient location, such as a private home, place of worship, community building, school, or library.

Anticrime programs achieve good results when citizens work with law enforcement agencies.

Invite a police or sheriff's officer to attend. The officer can offer an assessment of the problems in your community. Ask the police chief or sheriff for a letter of support to show the Neighborhood Watch members.

Design a flier or letter of invitation and deliver, with a parent or counselor, a copy to each home in your neighborhood. Follow up by calling or visiting the neighbors and reminding them of the meeting time and location. Try to have each household agree to send at least one adult member to the meeting. Senior citizens, especially those who are retired, are an asset to a Neighborhood Watch program. Because they might be home more often, they can watch the neighborhood when other adults are at work and children are at school.

Arrange to have refreshments, such as soft drinks and cookies, after the meeting.

Conducting the First Meeting

Members of the planning committee should arrive early to introduce the crime prevention officer and help everyone get acquainted.

Start the meeting with participants introducing themselves, sharing their concerns about crime in the neighborhood, and offering any ideas they have. Prepare and distribute an attendance sheet with each participant's address and phone number.

Ask the officer to give details on any part of the Neighborhood Watch program that might not be clear, such as training, signs, and other materials available. Some police departments, for example, have access to used mobile phones that are programmed for contacting only emergency services. Plus, ask for ideas about using two-way radios and uniforms. The officer could help develop safety patrols.

Discuss neighborhood crime statistics. When neighbors learn about crimes and suspicious incidents or activities in your neighborhood, they are more likely to make a strong commitment to the program.

Year to Date

Complaint	January-04	February-04	March-04	April-04	May-04	June-04	July-04	August-04
ASSAULT	72	45	72	54	71	50	53	61
BURGLARY OF BUILDING	53	48	33	64	56	74	59	79
BURGLARY IN PROGRESS	23	17	23	27	26	20	22	18
BURGLARY OF VEHICLE	82	69	142	99	141	112	71	109
CONTROLED SUBSTANCE	45	40	47	47	34	46	45	47
CRIMINAL MISCHIEF	94	119	127	138	131	96	92	105
DISTURBANCE DOMESTIC	186	211	181	138	164	164	207	195
DISTURBANCE MUSIC	234	248	268	302	238	187	185	19
DISTURBANCE OTHER	242	230	237	271	271	253	253	28
FIGHT	33	50	34	51	33	18	31	5
FORGERY	16	13	18	22	30	22	20	
LIQUOR LAW VIOLATION	12	5	20	14	11	17	25	
MTR VEH ACC HIT AND RUN	66	80	60	74	81	67	73	
MTR VEH ACC WITH INJURY	38	53	52	78	75	54	63	
MTR VEH ACC MINOR	195	264	243	270	247	242	218	
THEFT REPORT	170	211	231	245	220	240	257	
TOTAL CALLS	8058	7295	8283	8371	8398	7704	7938	7

Prepared By:
Eric Parkey

Dispatch Call Activity

Complaint	Year End 2002	Year End 2003
ASSAULT	1342	1256
BURGLARY OF BUILDING	1035	952
BURGLARY IN PROGRESS	885	
BURGLARY OF VEHICLE	1396	736
		1428
CONTROLED SUBSTANCE	1096	
CRIMINAL MISCHIEF	1799	1288
CRIMINAL TRESPASS	742	1722
		610
DISTURBANCE DOMESTIC		
DISTURBANCE MUSIC	5284	5270
DISTURBANCE OTHER	3548	3250
FIGHT	5227	5768
FORGERY	1509	1190
LIQUOR LAW VIOLA		
LOST PROPERTY		
MTR VEH ACC HIT A		
MTR VEH ACC WITH		
MTR VEH ACC MINC		
PERSON WITH GUN		
THEFT REPORT		

Prepared By: Eric Pa

Monthly Report -August 2004

Complaint	August-03	August-04	% Change
ASSAULT			
BURGLARY OF BUILDING	60	61	1.67
BURGLARY IN PROGRESS	73		
BURGLARY OF VEHICLE	18	79	8.22
CONTROLED SUBSTANCE	102	109	6.86
CRIMINAL MISCHIEF	38	47	23.68
DISTURBANCE DOMESTIC	117	105	-10.26
DISTURBANCE MUSIC	193	195	1.04
DISTURBANCE OTHER	319	193	-39.50
FIGHT	263	287	9.13
FORGERY	48	54	12.50
LIQUOR LAW VIOLATION	9	16	77.78
MTR VEH ACC HIT AND RUN	35	20	-42.86
MTR VEH ACC WITH INJURY	75	69	-8.00
MTR VEH ACC MINOR	67	51	-23.88
THEFT REPORT	250	226	-9.60
TOTAL CALLS	225	256	15.11
	8776	7986	-9.00

Your group should set an agenda and achievable goals, and establish a mission statement. Your crime prevention officer might help explain what the group can realistically expect to accomplish. Develop strategies for recruiting and involving a larger group of residents. Develop an action plan that identifies specific community changes and specifies who will perform each task. Set a timetable for each task and include people who have influence in the community.

The group probably will not agree on everything and there could be setbacks. But the group should be reminded that the program is for the safety and welfare of the neighborhood.

Discuss how the program will be coordinated:

- Explain the responsibilities of the Neighborhood Watch coordinator and block captains. (Their duties will be described later in this section.)

- Have nominations and elect people to fill the positions, or ask for volunteers to fill the positions. The group will need a secretary to record the minutes (activities) of the meetings and other events, and a treasurer, who will collect, record, and distribute funds.

- The group can collect membership dues and donations to raise funds for some projects.

- Establish committees, if possible, to involve more residents. These committees could be charged with inviting guest speakers, distributing fliers, and working on other events.

To maintain momentum for your Neighborhood Watch group, it is a good idea to schedule monthly meetings. Besides reviewing crime in the neighborhood, the meetings could be educational. There are many resources to tap. Federal, state, and local law enforcement and judicial agencies feature public affairs offices. Also, check with municipal or county agencies, as well as public works departments, hospitals, and public utilities, to see if they would provide information or speakers for future meetings.

While many adults might be fearful or uneasy about crime in their neighborhoods, the National Crime Prevention Council has found that many are willing to become active in their neighborhoods.

Program Coordination

Having individuals fill specific roles for your Neighborhood Watch program will help ensure its success.

Coordinator. The coordinator's responsibility is crucial to the success of the program. This might be a position for a retiree or other person who is often at home. Here are some responsibilities a coordinator might have.

- Maintain a current list of participants and neighborhood residents, including names, addresses, home and work telephone numbers, and vehicle descriptions. By having a list of neighborhood vehicles, it is easier to know when an outside vehicle is roaming the neighborhood.

- Expand the program to include more residents and act as a liaison between members, law enforcement officers, civic groups, and block captains.

- Arrange neighborhood crime prevention training programs.

- Obtain and distribute crime prevention materials, such as stickers and signs.

- Involve other volunteers to develop specific crime prevention projects to meet the community's needs.

- Encourage everyone in the neighborhood to participate in Operation Identification, a program in which personal property is marked with unique identifying numbers.

Block captains. The group should select one block captain for every 10 to 15 homes. Block captains work directly with their immediate neighbors. Here are some responsibilities a block captain might have:

- Serve as a liaison between block residents and the coordinator.

- Conduct home-security inspections.

- Organize foot, bicycle, mobile, and building patrols.

Recognizing Suspicious Activity

All block captains and patrollers need to know how to recognize suspicious activity. They need to be alert and notice anything that seems out of place or is happening at an unusual time. They should:

- Learn the techniques of obtaining an accurate description of a suspect and/or a vehicle and how to give an accurate description of the location.

- Know how to request assistance from police if anyone is threatened or in danger.

- Leave the investigation of suspicious activity or persons to law enforcement agents.

- Call the police or sheriff's department immediately instead of taking risks to try to prevent a crime. Block captains or members of a patrol should not be embarrassed if the suspicions prove wrong. Law enforcement officers would rather investigate than be called after it is too late.

Here are some incidents or activities that might be signs of a criminal activity and should be reported:

- Open or broken doors or windows at a closed business or an unoccupied residence.

- Sounds of breaking glass.

- Other unusual noises such as screaming, dogs barking continuously, or gunshots.

- Someone exhibiting unusual mental or physical symptoms that might indicate the person is injured, under the influence of drugs, or in need of medical attention.

- Continuous repair work at a nonbusiness location, suggesting that stolen property is being altered to prevent identification.

- Unusual chemical odors that could indicate illegal drug manufacturing.

Use your law enforcement agency's emergency number to report life-threatening incidents or a crime in progress. Use the nonemergency number for crimes that already have happened. Speed and accuracy are critical in reporting crimes or suspicious events. Your call could save a life or help prevent an injury or crime. The information that you provide will be kept confidential. You do not need to give your name, although this often is helpful.

Recognizing Suspicious Incidents

Not every stranger who comes into your neighborhood is a criminal. Trustworthy door-to-door salespersons and repair people often go into many residential areas. Occasionally, however, criminals disguise themselves as one of these workers. Therefore, it is important to be alert even to the activities of workers who seem legitimate.

Call law enforcement officers if you see someone:

- Behaving suspiciously, such as a person who goes to the rear of a residence or hangs around in front of an empty house or a closed business.

- Forcing his or her way into a house or entering an unoccupied residence.

- Running, but apparently not for exercise. If this person is carrying something of value or carrying unwrapped property at an unusual hour, it could suggest the person is fleeing the scene of a crime.

- Screaming.

- Standing around or peering into cars, especially in parking lots or on streets.

- Hanging around schools, parks, or secluded areas.

- Offering goods for sale at very low prices. The person might be trying to sell stolen goods.

- Loitering in or driving through a neighborhood several times.

- Seeming to be a delivery driver with a wrong address. It could be a burglar looking for an easy target.

Heavy traffic to and from a residence, particularly if it happens daily, also could indicate criminal activity, such as someone dealing in drugs or stolen property.

Recognizing Suspicious Vehicles

Call 9-1-1 immediately if you see someone, especially a child or woman, being forced into a vehicle. You could be witnessing a kidnapping, an assault, or other serious crime.

Vehicles in the following situations also may be involved in crimes and should be reported to authorities:

- Slow moving, without lights, and following an aimless course on residential streets, around schools, near playgrounds, or in any location.

- Parked and occupied by one or more persons, especially at an unusual hour, suggesting lookouts for a burglary or robbery.

- Parked near a closed business or an unoccupied residence and being loaded with valuables, suggesting burglary or theft.

- Abandoned in your neighborhood. It could possibly be a stolen car.

- Containing weapons.

- Being forcibly entered by someone, especially in a parking lot.

- Being stripped of parts or accessories.

- Having objects thrown from it, which possibly could be the disposing of illegal or stolen goods.

- Being used as a place for business dealings, especially around schools or parks, which suggests selling of drugs or stolen property.

Giving Descriptions

Practicing how to give quick, accurate descriptions is an excellent Neighborhood Watch meeting activity. To describe events, vehicles, or people precisely, write down the details of what you have seen while they are fresh in your mind. You want the descriptions that you will give to law enforcement officials to be as accurate as possible.

When describing an event, write down:

- The problem or what happened.

- Where it happened, which could include the street, nearest cross street, or address, or a landmark near the problem.

- Whether it is still happening, or when it occurred.

- Whether anyone is injured. Try to be as specific as possible; this information could save a life.

- How many people were or are involved.

- Whether there are weapons involved and, if so, what type.

- What the people involved look like, including sex, race, approximate age, approximate height, approximate weight and build, hair color and length, facial hair, eye color, complexion (light, dark, olive, ruddy), and type of clothes being worn. Did they have any peculiar or identifying mannerisms, physical disabilities, disfigurations, scars, tattoos, or voice characteristics? Was the person wearing glasses? Jewelry?

- If there are vehicles involved, write down the license number and the name of the state where the license plate was issued. Also, try to identify the make, model, year, and color of the vehicle.

- Any special designs or unusual features, such as a vinyl top, mag wheels, body damage, or pinstripes.

- The direction the people and/or vehicle headed.

- Your name, address, and telephone number.

It might help if you try to compare the weight and height of the person or people involved with your own or someone you know. Other information that could be helpful includes: What was said? What was taken? Were there other witnesses?

If patrol groups are organized, it is important that they work together. Patrols can share the same frequency if using walkie-talkies and/or go on joint patrols when necessary.

Benefits of Neighborhood Watch

1. Reduces and deters criminal activity.
2. Creates a greater sense of security among residents and reduces fear of crime.
3. Serves as an outlet for victims of crime.
4. Builds bonds with neighbors because residents look out for one another.
5. Reduces the risk of becoming a crime victim.
6. Instructs residents on how to observe and report suspicious activities.
7. Addresses quality-of-life issues and mutual interests in neighborhoods.

Group Projects

Here are some other projects, ideas, and program topics that your Neighborhood Watch group might want to consider.

Project Safe House

The Neighborhood Watch group could identify volunteer residences as "safe houses." These homes could be identified by bright stickers on windows and doors. These safe houses mean that people living there are "block parents" willing to help any child who is frightened or being chased.

Retired people or those who have a home business and are at home much of the day are well-suited to serve as block parents. Your group might encourage these members to make their homes "safe houses" or "block homes," where children can go for help. Law enforcement authorities should be aware of designated safe houses.

Youth Escort Service

A youth escort service is one way to assist older people. Through this service, organized by the Neighborhood Watch group, two young people go with an elderly person on regularly scheduled trips, or when the person phones in a request to a central escort service number.

A youth escort service is not a security or bodyguard service, but a program to ease the fears older people might have about crime. A person's fear of crime often is worse than the reality of the danger. Soothing this fear is a worthwhile service.

Crime Stoppers

The successful, nationwide Crime Stoppers program is based on the simple idea that for every crime committed, someone other than the offender has information that could solve the crime. Calls to Crime Stoppers are anonymous so that people can report a crime without fear of getting involved or having the criminal get revenge.

To ensure anonymity, callers reporting crimes are not asked to give their names. They are assigned code numbers, which are used in all future communications. If the caller's tip leads to an arrest and conviction, Crime Stoppers pays a reward.

Your Neighborhood Watch group can help start a Crime Stoppers program in your area or contribute to an existing one by encouraging public, law enforcement, and media support.

Seasonal Crime Prevention Tips

Crime tips are a way your group can give timely information to neighbors during holidays, special events, or different seasons of the year. Examples of seasonal crime prevention tips include advising Christmas shoppers to lock packages in the trunk of their cars rather than leaving them in view on the seat, or to offer summer vacationers tips on home security while they are away.

The program can be done inexpensively. Your group simply could print seasonal crime prevention tips on a postcard and mail or hand them out throughout the community. Or, you might provide tips in the form of public service announcements on local radio and television stations.

Telephone Trees

Telephone trees can help neighbors quickly reach each other with emergency information. Neighborhoods are divided into small, workable areas, by streets or along natural boundaries. Each neighborhood group prepares a chart that has the names and phone numbers of all members.

Each group chooses a block captain or other person for the police or sheriff's office to contact with important information. Every person on the telephone tree knows which neighbor or neighbors to call when there is emergency information or other communications to pass along in a hurry.

Mobilizing Scanner Owners

Owners of emergency radio scanners can play a vital role as additional eyes and ears for the local enforcement agencies and Neighborhood Watch groups. Because scanner owners receive information immediately, they can instantly warn members of their crime prevention group about emergencies in their neighborhoods.

Beautification Projects

Your group could organize a project to remove trash, abandoned autos, and other unsightly nuisances from your neighborhood. Working to make a neighborhood more attractive and livable builds community pride. Research has shown that these kinds of improvements can reduce crime and lower the fear of crime in a community.

Fire Prevention Programs

Fire prevention and other safety-related programs can be excellent topics for your Neighborhood Watch meetings. Your group could invite fire prevention officers to give programs on such subjects as cardiopulmonary resuscitation, disaster preparedness, and fire safety.

Operation Fingerprint

Thousands of children are reported missing every year. Fingerprinting children can help to identify them. Law enforcement departments throughout the United States are fingerprinting children at no cost to parents. Neighborhood Watch parents can participate in this effort and encourage others to participate.

Drug Awareness

The U.S. government spends billions of taxpayer dollars every year to combat illegal drugs. The crimes associated with drugs go beyond the sale and use of the illegal substances. Some drug users steal from others to get the money they need to buy illegal drugs. While under the influence of drugs, users may commit violent crimes, including assault and murder. Drug dealers often resort to violence to protect their illegal business.

Programs exist to help you get the message about drugs to your friends. The programs at many schools and communities include the Partnership for a Drug-Free America, Drug Abuse Resistance Education, LifeSkills® Training, and the Boy Scouts of America's "Drugs: A Deadly Game" campaign. This prevention and awareness program stimulates discussion in small groups and in classrooms about the dangers of drug abuse.

> You can help run drug dealers out of business by not doing drugs, by helping friends either stay off or refuse drugs, and by reporting dealers to police.

Gateway Drugs

Nicotine, alcohol, and marijuana are sometimes described as gateway drugs. That is because these drugs are addictive, and their use can be a gateway to the use of other drugs. Though substance abuse does not necessarily lead to delinquent behavior, the two are strongly linked.

A national crime victimization survey found that 5.3 million violent acts were committed against people 12 years old and up. Among these victims of violence, 29 percent said that the offender was using drugs, sometimes along with alcohol.

Nicotine, one of the main chemical components of tobacco, is a habit-forming drug. A person can become chemically dependent on nicotine either by smoking or using tobacco in other forms. The health problems associated with smoking cigarettes include lung cancer, cardiovascular and respiratory diseases, and burns. Breathing in second-hand smoke, or smoke from someone else's cigarette, also has been attributed to some of these diseases.

Young people who drink are more likely to be victims of violent crime, including rape, aggravated assault, and robbery. Also, teens who drink are more likely to have behavior and academic problems.

Like nicotine, alcohol also is legal for adults and addictive, and it can destroy the health of people who abuse it. Drinking too much alcohol impairs the ability to speak clearly, control body movements, or drive a car safely. Nearly 20,000 deaths are caused each year by drunken drivers. Alcohol not only affects the mind and body, it also causes a lack of judgment and coping skills. It remains the No. 1 drug of choice among teens.

Marijuana, also called "weed," "pot," and "hash," among many other names, can be addictive. Many scientists classify the drug as hallucinogenic, which means it plays tricks on the mind and causes users to experience things that are not real. Marijuana disrupts the way the brain handles thoughts and emotions. Users find it difficult to think clearly, pay attention, do ordinary tasks, and remember things. Possessing, using, or selling marijuana is against the law in the United States.

The National Institute on Drug Abuse reports that marijuana use by children results in lower achievement than nonusers, acceptance of deviant behavior, and aggression.

Uppers, Downers, and Club Drugs

In addition to gateway drugs, more dangerous and addictive chemicals and drugs are illegally used every day. These types of substances should be avoided at all costs.

Inhalants are substances such as model airplane glue, lacquer thinner, lighter fluid, and propellants from aerosol cans such as deodorant, hair spray, canned whipped topping, and cleaning fluids.

Some people will sniff these cheap and easily available chemicals to get high and to win approval from their peers. However, serious health consequences can result. Even a single session of repeated inhalant abuse can disrupt heart rhythms and cause death. Regular abuse can result in serious harm to vital organs, including the brain, heart, kidneys, and liver.

When properly prescribed by a physician, tranquilizers are legal drugs. However, when abused or combined with alcohol or other depressants, they can be dangerous. Abuse of tranquilizers can cause poor coordination, slurred speech, tremors, nausea, mood swings, confusion, nightmares, and possibly coma.

> The National Institute of Drug Abuse reports that approximately 20 percent of eighth-graders have abused inhalants. A national survey on drug use and health shows that more than 2.6 million youths, ages 12 to 17, have used inhalants at least once.

Besides marijuana, hallucinogens or psy-chedelic drugs include LSD (or "acid," which is its more common street name), Ecstasy (XTC), PCP (also known as "angel dust," "ozone," and "wack"), mescaline, and psilocybin. These drugs produce unpredictable effects, ranging from hallucinations to convulsions. Users can die from severe convulsions, overdose, and the mixing of hallucinogens.

Designer or club drugs such as AMF ("China white") and MPTP ("new heroin") often take the form of a white powder meant to resemble heroin. Designer drugs are meant to mimic the effects of illegal drugs. They depress the body's circulation and respiratory systems and can lead to death. Ecstasy and PCP are examples of designer drugs.

Cocaine (also called "coke," "C," "flake," "snow," and "stardust") stimulates the central nervous system and, besides causing a euphoric condition, can cause strong psychological dependence. Bizarre behavior while under the influence of cocaine can unwittingly lead to fatal accidents and to violence such as suicide or murder. Freebasing (heating cocaine to dissolve it) often causes severe burn accidents.

Crack cocaine (also known as "crack," "rock," and "readyrock") is cocaine that has been processed from cocaine hydrochloride to a freebase for smoking. The term "crack" refers to the crackling sound heard when the mixture is heated ("smoked").

Common names for heroin include "dust," "H," "horse," "junk," and "smack." A user becomes dependent even with occasional abuse and in low doses. Effects of heroin include irregular breathing and heartbeat. Slowed breathing can lead to brain damage. Death often results from the fatal lung and heart complications caused by overdoses.

Narcotics include codeine, methadone, morphine, and other painkillers. Their use is illegal unless prescribed by a licensed physician. Narcotics depress breathing and all body systems. Users risk the dangerous impurity of street drugs and the hazards of needle use (including AIDS infections). Overdoses and taking narcotics with other drugs that have depressing effects on the body can be fatal.

Amphetamines have names such as "speed," "meth," "methamphetamine," "wire," "bennies," "black beauties," "copilots," "dexies," and "uppers." These drugs overstimulate and overwork the body, causing a fast and irregular heartbeat and breathing, severe depression, and paranoia. Users can die from the collapse of blood vessels in the brain and from heart failure.

> While under the influence of amphetamines, users can engage in violent behavior; the depression the drugs cause can lead to suicide. Studies have shown that the use of speed is associated with more violence and antisocial behavior than any other illegal drug.

Names for barbiturates include "barbs," "downers," and "ludes." Barbiturates are legal when medically prescribed. Abusers risk life-threatening complications and severe withdrawal symptoms. Death can result from stopped breathing, lethal combinations with other drugs such as alcohol, extreme withdrawal reactions, and suicide.

Anabolic steroids are synthetic substances related to the male sex hormone testosterone, which controls the development of masculine traits. Some athletes have abused steroids in an effort to enhance their performance and physical build. Long-term users can become dependent. Steroid abusers risk cancer or severe damage of the liver, reproductive organs, and cardiovascular system.

Studies show that increased aggression may result from abuse of anabolic steroids.

Child Abuse

With nearly a million children victimized annually by some type of mistreatment, child abuse is a major problem for our nation. Of these children, more than half are victims of neglect; 2 percent are medically neglected; 19 percent are physically abused; 10 percent are sexually abused; and 7 percent are psychologically mistreated. However, these numbers probably are low because there is no way of knowing how many crimes against children are never reported.

> Each year, an estimated 1,300 children die in the United States as a result of abuse or neglect.

Most of us can recognize bruises and other possible signs of physical abuse. But there are cases of abuse that are not so noticeable, such as sexual abuse by a family member or a friend, emotional maltreatment, and, in some cases, physical abuse that happens behind closed doors and can be hidden by clothing.

To stop child abuse, it must first be identified. If someone tries to abuse you or touch you in a way that makes you feel uncomfortable, yell "No!" Get away from the person and tell a trusted adult. If you have a friend who shows any indicators of abuse, that friend might need your help in reporting the abuse.

The U.S. Department of Health and Human Services lists these signs to look for in a child who is suffering from abuse or neglect.

- Sudden changes in behavior or school performance
- Physical or medical problems brought to a parent's attention have been ignored
- Learning problems
- Pessimistic outlook on life, often expecting something terrible to happen
- Lack of adult supervision
- Overly passive or withdrawn
- Arrives for school or activities early, stays late, and does not want to go home

Signs of physical abuse include unexplained bruises, broken bones, black eyes, burns, or appearing to be fearful of parents. Signs of neglect could include frequent absence from school, begging or stealing money or food, lack of medical or dental care, poor personal hygiene, lack of proper clothing for the weather, and abuse of alcohol or other drugs.

Signs of sexual abuse in a victim include:

- Having difficulty walking or sitting
- Refusing to change clothes for gym or other physical activities
- Reporting nightmares or bedwetting
- Having a sudden change in appetite
- Demonstrating unusual sexual knowledge or behavior
- Contracting a venereal disease

Signs of emotional mistreatment in a victim might include

- Extremes in behavior
- Delayed physical or emotional development
- Threats or attempts of suicide
- Displaying a lack of attachment to the parent or parents

Children's lives can depend on caring citizens who recognize and report signs of abuse. Report any suspicions to your parents or school official. If your suspicions are correct, you could be giving your friend the only chance he or she has of growing up healthy. You could even save your friend's life.

Since 1985, the BSA has emphasized the prevention of child abuse. Materials that you should be familiar with include section II of *How to Protect Your Children From Child Abuse: A Parent's Guide* in the front of each *Boy Scout Handbook,* the section on child abuse in the "Personal Development" chapter of the *Boy Scout Handbook,* and the video *A Time to Tell.* These resources introduce the three R's of BSA Youth Protection (Recognize, Resist, Report).

Scouts need to recognize situations that can place them at risk of being molested; they need to know that if they resist, most child molesters will leave them alone; and they should report any attempt of molestation to help protect themselves and others.

Roles of Police and Sheriff's Departments

Cities hire and train police to help uphold the law and to apprehend those who break it. Many police officers work with residents of the community to help prevent crime by supporting programs such as Neighborhood Watch. Police often are involved in programs at schools to help alleviate juvenile crime by interacting with youths.

A sheriff's department usually is headed by a sheriff elected by residents of a county. Besides law enforcement duties, sheriffs' roles can include operating a jail, providing courthouse security, serving various types of civil court papers, collecting taxes, and, in some cities, providing police services.

Crime Prevention Agencies

Discuss with your counselor the purposes and operations of agencies that are involved in crime prevention and those that help victims deal with crime. If possible, visit one agency's headquarters and speak to an official. Find out how the work done by that agency helps to prevent crime and helps victims. Explain the relationship between the agency and the criminal justice system. Learn how that agency works with law enforcement agencies in emergencies.

Depending on the size of your community, you might find listings in the telephone book for the police and sheriff's departments, alcohol- and drug-abuse counseling, Crime Stoppers, FBI, U.S. Marshal, Secret Service, youth and abuse hotlines, crisis intervention hotlines, shelters for battered spouses, and victim assistance agencies.

The Role of Private Security

Private security officers are not law enforcement officers and usually do not have the same authority. They typically are hired by businesses, individuals, or institutions to protect everything from assets to lives. Although there are a few exceptions, most private security officers are not permitted by law to arrest anyone.

Private security is a big business with about 2 million persons employed as officers.

You probably have seen private security officers at museums, retail stores, office buildings, concerts, sports venues, and airports. At many office buildings, for example, workers must show an identification card to a private security officer before being allowed to enter the building. Roles of the officers, then, include enforcing rules of the individual or business that hired them, controlling access to an employer's property, preventing loss or theft of property, managing traffic flow, and deterring criminal activity on the property.

Careers in Crime Prevention and Security

Because crime continues to be a major problem, a variety of career possibilities exist in law enforcement and security. Opportunities can be found at the federal, state, and local levels.

Law enforcement agencies include police, sheriff, highway patrol, Drug Enforcement Agency, FBI, Secret Service, and U.S. Marshal. You also could pursue a career as private security guard, private investigator, corrections officer, airport security officer, attorney, judge, or forensics expert.

At a minimum, these positions require a high school diploma; many require a college degree. In addition, many agencies have their own training programs.

There also are positions for those interested in computer security. People in this field help to enforce security on the Internet by thwarting con artists, hackers, embezzlers, child pornographers, and other criminals engaged in illegal activities.

Crime Prevention Resources

Scouting Literature

Drugs: A Deadly Game pamphlet;
Citizenship in the Community,
Citizenship in the Nation,
Fingerprinting, Fire Safety, Law, and
Safety merit badge pamphlets

Visit the Boy Scouts of America's
official retail Web site at *http://
www.scoutstuff.org* for a complete
listing of all merit badge pamphlets
and other helpful Scouting materials and supplies.

Books

Davidson, Tom, et al. *The Complete
Idiot's Guide to Home Security.*
Alpha Books, 2001.

DeBecker, Gavin. *Protecting the Gift:
Keeping Children and Teenagers Safe
(and Parents Sane).* Dell, 2000.

Giggans, Patricia Occhiuzzo, and Barrie
Levy. *50 Ways to a Safer World:
Everyday Actions You Can Take to
Prevent Violence in Neighborhoods,
Schools, and Communities.* Seal
Press, 1997.

Hammer, Carl. *Home Security: How to
Select Reliable Locks and Alarms for*
Your Home, Office, or Car. Paladin
Press, 2001.

Kraizer, Sherryll. *The Safe Child Book:
A Commonsense Approach to
Protecting Children and Teaching
Children to Protect Themselves.*
Fireside, 1996.

Mann, Stephanie, et al. *Safe Homes,
Safe Neighborhoods: Stopping Crime
Where You Live.* Nole Press, 1993.

Rawls, Neal, and Sue Kovach. *Be
Alert, Be Aware, Have a Plan: The
Complete Guide to Personal Security.*
The Lyons Press, 2002.

Sherman, Josepha. *Internet Safety.*
Franklin Watts, 2003.

Organizations and Web Sites

Bureau of Justice Assistance
U.S. Department of Justice
Telephone: 202-616-6500
Web site: *http://www.ojp.usdoj.gov*

Crime Prevention Through Environmental Design
International CPTED Association
Web site: *http://www.cpted.net*

National Center for Missing & Exploited Children
Toll-free hotline: 800-843-5678
Web site: *http://www.missingkids.com*

National Child Identification Program

Toll-free telephone: 888-55-IDKIT
Web site: *http://www. childidprogram.com*

National Committee to Prevent Child Abuse

Telephone: 312-663-3520
Web site: *http://www.childabuse.org*

National Crime Prevention Council

Telephone: 202-466-6272
Web site: *http://www.ncpc.org*

National McGruff House Network

Telephone: 801-486-8691
Web site: *http://www.mcgruff.org*

National School Safety Center

Telephone: 805-373-9977
Web site: *http://www.nssc1.org*

National Sheriffs' Association

Telephone: 703-836-7827
Web site: *http://www.sheriffs.org*

Youth Crime Watch of America

Telephone: 305-670-2409
Web site: *http://www.ycwa.org*

Acknowledgments

The Boy Scouts of America thanks Joanne McDaniel, director, and William Lassiter, school safety specialist, the Center for the Prevention of School Violence, North Carolina Department of Juvenile Justice and Delinquency Prevention. Ms. McDaniel and Mr. Lassiter (who also is an Eagle Scout) helped revise the Crime Prevention merit badge requirements.

We appreciate the Quicklist Consulting Committee of the Association for Library Service to Children, a division of the American Library Association, for its assistance with updating the resources section of this merit badge pamphlet.

Photo Credits

©Photos.com—cover *(shoplifter sign, police scanner, security camera, fire alarm, police patch, warning sign, dog, button, lock and key);* pages 11–12 *(both),* 14 *(background),* 15, 16 *(background),* 21, 28, 42–46 *(all),* 51–52 *(both),* 59, and 62 *(background)*

All other photos not mentioned above are the property of or are protected by the Boy Scouts of America.

Jack Brown—page 19

Dan Bryant—pages 31–32 *(both),* 41, and 47

Frank McMahon—page 50

Brian Payne—pages 8 and 13 *(top)*

Randy Piland—page 14 *(inset)*

Doug Wilson—cover *(Neighborhood Watch sign);* page 7